FOREVER KING

Surviving the Loss of My Unborn Child

DIANA SIMS

Copyright © 2017 by Diana Sims

All rights reserved. This book or any portion thereof may not be reproduced or used in any manner whatsoever without the express written permission of the publisher except for the use of brief quotations in a book review.

ISBN: 978-06928469-8-8

Library of Congress Control Number: 2017902861

Edited by: Michelle Otis

Cover Design: Knowledge Power Communications, Inc.

Unless otherwise indicated, all scriptural references are taken from the King James Version.

For more information, contact:
Forever King Publishing
Diana Sims
Contact#:866-951-KING (5464)
KingJosiahSims@gmail.com
www.Foreverking.us
Twitter/Facebook/Instagram: Foreverking2014
Blog: www.foreverking2014.wordpress.com
First Printed, 2017

Printed in the United States of America

Inspirational Scriptures

Isaiah 40:31

"But they that wait upon the LORD shall renew their strength; they shall mount up with wings as eagles; they shall run, and not be weary; and they shall walk, and not faint."

Isaiah 43:2

"When thou passest through the waters, I will be with thee; and through the rivers, they shall not overflow thee: when thou walkest through the fire, thou shalt not be burned; neither shall the flame kindle upon thee."

Proverbs 3:5

"Trust in the LORD with all thine heart; and lean not unto thine own understanding."

2 Corinthians 1:3-4

"Blessed be God, even the Father of our Lord Jesus Christ, the Father of mercies, and the God of all comfort; ^{4} Who comforteth us in all our tribulation, that we may be able to comfort them which are in any trouble, by the comfort wherewith we ourselves are comforted of God."

Psalm 56:8

"You keep track of all my sorrows. You have collected all my tears in your bottle. You have recorded each one in your book."

Romans 8:18

For I reckon that the sufferings of this present time are not worthy to be compared with the glory which shall be revealed in us.

Dedication

This book is dedicated to my husband, Cory. I love you! You were my strength during this season of our lives. I am forever grateful to you!

To my boys, Isaiah and Solomon, for loving me unconditionally, praying for me, and showing me that life is worth fighting for.

To my newest addition, Anthony, my rainbow baby after a devastating loss and the storm.

To my beautiful mother, Golden Lady with angel kisses named Phyllis, who is my rock, prayer warrior, and dreamer, a true intercessor who interceded and travailed for me when I was just three months old. I wasn't supposed to have made it, but by the grace of God and her persistence in her confessions of my healing, I am here today. I love you so much!

To my birth father, Elbert, without you I would not be here or have part of me that is ever-present. Thank you for the gifts, my tribe of brothers and sisters (Freeman Kids), and your face (smile). I love you!

To my dad, Colemon, words cannot express the respect and appreciation I have for you and how God saw fit to drop you down from heaven to be my earthly father, whom I've longed for my entire life. I love you so much!

To My brother, Robert, my number one fan. You have so much to do and to accomplish on this earth. Your gifts will make room for your story and the gift of song will be heard. Keep the faith. I love you!

To all the mothers and fathers who have suffered the loss of a child, I feel your pain. I've been there, and I know where you can go if you believe life can go on.

Last, but not least, I dedicate this book to my unborn son, King Josiah Sims. Rest in Paradise, love - Forever King.

King Josiah Sims

"Mommy loves you,"
I would say to my baby King
Early each morning
After I would pray and sing

Mommy loves you Josiah
Hebrew for "God will save"
On July the 5th, you went home
Back to heaven to protect us; you're so brave

Mommy loves you baby Sims
Nine months I carried you in my womb
From the first heartbeat to the last
Every turn, kick, and punch in my memories speaks volumes.

Mommy loves you, King Josiah Sims
Today we lay your body to rest
Tell Jehovah Jireh to take care of you
My little angel, you are blessed.

Table of Contents

Dedication vii

Introduction xiii

Chapter 1: Third Trimester Tragedy 1

Chapter 2: Grieving the Loss of King.. 11

Chapter 3: Pregnancy after Stillbirth... 21

Chapter 4: Forever King! A Strategy of Survival........................... 27

Chapter 5: Suffering the Loss of an Unborn or Stillborn Child 33

Chapter 6: The Importance of Prayer for Grieving Mothers 37

Chapter 7: Studying the Word of God 41

Chapter 8: God's Sovereignty in Times of Grief 45

Chapter 9: The Experience of Joy as Commanded by God 49

Chapter 10: The Intervention of a Support Group 51

Forever King.. 55

Acknowledgements 57

About the Author.. 59

Introduction

God gave me the desire to share my story late one evening. I thought about it to the point I was not able to fall asleep. Some questions came to mind, because this part of my life was so precious, so sacred, so personal. How I could bare myself to the world and be transparent with the fear of rejection, judgment, or not understanding the level of grief I shared?

As I said all of these statements in my mind, I kept hearing, "Forever King, Forever King, and Forever King!" I finally went to sleep around midnight. I slept for a few hours and was awakened by my alarm. I know that my Heavenly Father, my Abba Father, my Yahweh, Yahovah, my Daddy, my Papa touched my spirit and said, "Diana, wake up. Live and pursue your purpose for this day." I woke up and began the beautiful gift called the "present."

I saw my phone had the text notification light on, so I checked it, and I had received a message that morning saying,

"God said: Write your book to help those who have suffered a loss and who will face the loss to heal." I looked up towards the sky and smiled and whispered to God, "You are something special!"

If we are obedient, God is able to deposit a priceless gift into our spirit, and if we pursue His purposes for us instead of over-analyzing the desire and/or word spoken as a confirmation, we can move mountains with hope!

So, take this book, go to a special place—your secret place—your car, your bedroom, your prayer closet, the park, or whatever place brings you solace and peace. Take your time reading this book. Take notes, highlight, underline, and pray about anything that stands out to you, because it is God speaking to you through me. I want to be the one about whom you can say, "She introduced me to love, peace, hope, and her Heavenly Father."

The ultimate seed I carried for a season of my life was sown into fertile ground on July 21, 2014. The grief I experienced during the waiting period of the seed planted was at times overpowering. Nonetheless, all the tears I cried were not in vain. My tears watered and nurtured my seed until the appointed time. When the earth yielded my increase, King had a conversation with my Heavenly Father, and it went something like this...

Daddy; I want nothing but the best for my mommy, who will you send? I need him to look just like me so you can grant her request to see my eyes. I know, and she knows the precious soul you will send will not be me, but he will be exactly what my family needs. Let his eyes captivate all he comes across, let his smile light up the room, and let his touch melt the pain away. Give him a heart like David, strength like Samson, wisdom like Solomon, ears to hear You like Samuel, give him dreams like Joseph, and put a word in his mouth for this season like Isaiah and Jeremiah. Then God said to King, "I know exactly who to send, then He said, "Anthony, are you ready?" Anthony then replied, "Yes, here I am Dad, I'm ready to make her heart smile."

CHAPTER 1

Third Trimester Tragedy

It all started on Thursday, July 3, 2014. I remember it like it was yesterday. It was a beautiful summer day, clear skies, and a nice, very much appreciated breeze from the close by Santa Monica Pier. As I traveled on foot to my 36-week checkup and ultrasound, the nurse assigned to me that day gave me a biophysical profile (ultrasound and nonstress test combined) that was sent via live-feed to my doctor to view.

My baby King opened his hand and closed his hand as if he was saying, "Hello." The doctor was astonished. She said that babies at 36 weeks' gestation usually didn't have those motor skills yet. She said everything looked great and made my appointment for the following week. Little did I know that King was really saying, "Goodbye," and that would be the last time I saw him alive. I walked back to the office and stayed until the end of my modified shift. I gave hugs to everyone since I was starting maternity leave the next day.

On Friday, the 4th of July, 2014, hubby and the boys went to Bakersfield for the 4th of July festivities. I stayed home since I was so close to my due date. Instead of watching fireworks, I rested most of the day and then attempted to do some online shopping with a ToysRUs® gift card I had received from my coworkers.

I found a cute outfit that had a crown and the wording "King" on it, and I said this would be so cute since my husband had named our son King. For some reason, their system was having issues and would not complete the order. So, I mustered up some energy and took my pregnant self to Target to get some baby clothes for King.

As I was walking around in the store, I felt King getting heavy and felt that he was finally turned over and engaged since he was still breech during the ultrasound the previous day. On my way home, I grabbed some food, arrived home safely, and left the clothes in my trunk so Cory and the boys could bring them up the next day when they got home.

It was so hot, I had the central air on full-blast trying to cope with the heat since I was heavily pregnant. Neighbors far off were having fun with their families setting off fireworks. Cory and our two boys Isaiah and Solomon were still in Bakersfield having a ball with the family.

Cory and the boys were scheduled to come home from Bakersfield on the afternoon of July 5, 2014. Instead, he said he had an urge to come home in the early hours of July 5, 2014 since he knew King Josiah "KJ" was due soon. He kissed me, letting me know he was there, and I fell back to sleep.

It was around 8:40 a.m., and I noticed that "KJ" didn't wake me up with his usual happy kicking and moving around early in the morning.

I got up to use the bathroom, and as I wiped, this time it was different. There was dark blood on my tissue. I immediately screamed "CORY, I'm bleeding!" Cory immediately ran over and assured me it was okay and I explained to him in a cry of panic that I never bled before with either of the other boys. He put some of his basketball shorts on me. He grabbed our boys from out of their sleep, and we headed to the car. As we walked down the hall heading to the elevator, I told him to go back and get the car seat in case we were having King today. He ran back and grabbed it out of the box, and we were on our way.

Cory asked what he should do, since we had planned to have the baby at UCLA Ronald Regan Hospital in Westwood, and we lived in the San Fernando Valley. I explained I didn't want to drive beyond 30 minutes to get out to Westwood, so I instructed him to go to West Hills Hospital.

We arrived in the emergency room, and they asked how long I had been carrying the pregnancy. I replied, "Thirty-six weeks and two days." They checked me in, and a nurse immediately grabbed some big forceps to try to locate the bleeding, however, all her efforts proved unsuccessful. So, she hooked up the baby heart monitor against me and was searching for his heartbeat. As she was doing this, we both saw my stomach moving. She said that his heart was beating with as a regular a rhythm as mine, and I explained to her that it was absolutely ridiculous. She got another nurse claiming that she was good at locating active baby's heartbeats. The nurse observed that he was moving, so she immediately placed an order for an ultrasound. I told Cory to take the boys to a Subway™ restaurant that was across the street so they could get something to eat.

The technician came in and started performing the ultrasound. I noticed she was taking a lot of pictures, and I asked if he was still breech, and she affirmatively replied, "Yes." She left the room saying she needed to show the on-call doctor the results. She came back shortly and gave me a warm blanket and left again. Shortly after, a phlebotomist came in and said she needed to get my blood count. I questioned her, because I had stopped bleeding. When they did this before, it was just before I delivered my previous sons by caesarean section, and I did not want a stranger to deliver my baby. I only wanted my doctor. She replied, "Let me get the doctor."

The doctor came in and introduced herself. She asked for my husband, and I replied that he was across the street getting the boys something to eat. She said she wanted to wait until he got back, but I bluntly told her, "I am the mother. Is there something wrong?" She sat on the side of my bed, touched my leg, and simply said, "The baby passed away."

I looked at her in total disbelief. This was a dream, a nightmare, a sick joke. This could not be happening to me. I am a child of God. I serve at my church, I was on the prayer team and in the choir, I attended services, and I was faithful with my tithes and offerings. I attended all conferences. I was a good person. *I wanted my son!*

I was just laid off after 11 years, now this. I asked, "God, how could this happen? I prayed. I sought after you. I read my Bible. I ministered to others who had issues with getting pregnant or issues concerning their pregnancies, and you brought them through. You helped those I prayed for conceive and now this?" I didn't get it.

The only thing I could say at that moment was, "Jesus! That can't be possible! The other two nurses saw my stomach moving, and I could feel him moving." The doctor said it was the amniotic fluid moving him around. I just sat there in shock and called Cory. I told him he needed to come back now. He said he was downstairs putting the car seat in the car. I told him to stop and come up now. My heart was beating so fast.

I called my mother who was on the way to visit her sister in Menifee, California. I told her that King had passed away, and she said she was on her way.

After a few minutes, Cory came back with the boys. The nurse from the Neonatal Intensive Care Unit took the boys with her. Cory asked about the situation, and I looked him straight in the eyes and said, "King is gone." He immediately screamed, and tears dripped from his eyes like a flood. He socked the wall and then fell with his back against it. He pulled himself together and then came over to me.

The on-call doctor informed me she paged my doctor and was waiting to hear back. She asked if I wanted to deliver the baby at the West Hills Hospital or to be transported to UCLA in Westwood to have my doctor get it done.

I was about to say that since I was already there… At that moment, my doctor's call came in. She, too, was in disbelief. She had said the baby was fine two days prior. She asked if I still wanted to attempt to deliver the baby naturally since it would be an easier recovery, and I could make an appointment on Monday. I said that I did not want to continue to carry my baby who was no longer with me or try to have him by VBAC (vaginal birth after caesarean) since he was lifeless and could not assist with the process of delivery.

The on-call doctor admitted me at West Hills Hospital and awaited the anesthesiologist's arrival.

My mom arrived with dark shades on and sniffling.

My bloodwork was taken. The anesthesiologist came in and was calm and happy. My husband didn't care too much for his enthusiasm due to the circumstances, and they got into an argument. I stopped it by telling my husband to let him do his job. They walked me back to prep me for the caesarean. Once I was prepped for surgery, my husband came in.

As they were taking King out, they said the umbilical cord was wrapped around his neck tightly three times. Tears came streaming down from Cory's eyes. He saw our lifeless son's body being pulled out of me. He left my side to go to King. At this point, I had not seen him yet, since they were closing me back up.

After I completed my first part of recovery in the operating room, I was placed back into the room I was in earlier, and they sat me up. The recovery nurse asked if I wanted to see King. With tears in my eyes I answered, "I can see him?" I didn't know if that was an option. They had wrapped him up in a blanket as if he was alive and put a hat on him and handed to me. I didn't expect him to be a full-sized baby.

He was beautiful. He was 6 lbs., 19½ inches long and as I said, he was beautiful. As I held him, I told him that I loved him. I could see the welts on his neck from the umbilical cord that was around it. His mouth was open, and blood streamed down his nose. I panicked and said I couldn't hold him anymore.

My mom put him in the bassinet next to me. I asked her to take a picture, and she did. I could not move or walk around due to the epidural. As she was taking pictures, I silently pleaded with God and said, "As you did for women and their children in the Bible who had passed away, I still believe you can do it for my son." So, I whispered quietly, "King get up. King, King, I need you to wake up for Mommy. Please, wake up." However, nothing happened.

The nurse came in and asked if I wanted pictures of him, and she rolled him in the bathroom and took some pictures. She then brought him back to me. I told him bye and that I loved him. The nurse rolled him out. She returned with a beautiful keepsake with his information, his footprints, a lock of his hair, and the pictures she took of him.

I was sent off to Postpartum, of all places. A butterfly ribbon was placed on my door to notify anyone that came to the room that my baby was gone. There was one nurse who didn't notice as she came to take my vitals. She took my vitals and said to me, "Take your prenatal vitamin." I asked her, "Why?" She just stared at me. I said, "My baby is dead." She put it back and said she was sorry and left immediately.

I did not want the boys to see the baby so they kept them in the NICU. They brought them in later. However, Cory and I told them King had passed because they asked after the baby. They were confused and cried.

I started getting all these text messages and calls, and I was concerned. I didn't know that Cory had posted a picture of himself crying saying, "R.I.P. King."

My brother Bert came with Felicia, and she consoled me and told me about her experience. Bert gave me the biggest hug.

I asked my mom for my Bible after they left. I tried to read it, but I could barely see the words as tears continued to flow. So, I closed it and tried to sleep, but that was not successful. I was scared to go to sleep. I was in so much pain because the medicine had worn off, all I could do was to hold my stomach. This was so difficult for me. I was happy when my cousin Tameka and Aunt Deen showed up to visit me, even though I said I didn't want anyone there.

My cousin Tameka took the boys for a week to allow them not to be in the midst of the fresh tragic event that took place.

That evening, my mom relieved Cory so he could go home and get everything removed from the house. She stayed with me, and we had a brief conversation. I asked her, with tears coming down my eyes, "I don't understand. What was the point?" She responded, "Daughter, I don't know why this is a part of our journey, but I know God will get the glory out of it."

It was so hard for me to fall asleep. I was scared. I was paranoid. I was thinking about my son who was in a cold place no longer living. My mom lay in the bed next to me, and I finally fell asleep. She said she heard me sniffling, and it was hard for me to go to sleep with the sleep aid prescription.

She began to pray, read scriptures, and sing worship songs until she heard me snoring lightly. As I recovered at the hospital, my mom got me up walking the next morning. Because of the surgery, the doctor insisted that I get up and walk around to prevent blood clots in my legs. As I walked around in a circle in the hall holding onto my mother, I heard babies crying. I heard families celebrating, even singing "Happy Birthday" to their newborn children. I saw the nurses looking at me with empathy. All I wanted to do was to get back in the bed.

An older lady said, "Congratulations," as I walked past, and I shook my head and looked down. My mom told her that King passed, and I began to sob uncontrollably as she held me up.

Little did I know, while my mom was being strong for me on the outside, after she assisted me back to my bed, she went outside of my room, shut the door, and cried uncontrollably to the point where a nurse went to her with tissue.

I was so lost in my sorrows that I didn't realize how much the loss impacted her. My husband brought my bag to the room so I could have clothes, etc…and I told him to take the baby's clothes out of my bag, so he did. The director of the West Hills Hospital brought me a list of places where the baby's body could be deposited (mortuaries) and said we needed to figure out what we were going to do. They needed to know when he would be transported to the place of my choice.

Here I was grieving about not having a baby, and now I had to bury him. In the state of California, once the baby is past 24-weeks' gestation, the parents are responsible for the remains of their child and have to either bury or cremate the baby.

I had no money. My husband said he would take care of it, assuring me that we weren't going to "burn" our son. Later, he went to Home Depot® and rented a small truck. Cory went home and took down all the baby furniture and unopened boxes and put them into a storage so I wouldn't see them when I got home. I can't imagine the pain and heartache he was going through trying to do all these things and stay strong for me.

During my stay in the hospital, one of my nurses shared her story of losing a child. She came in and talked to me as she took my vitals and said, "I know you are hurting, but I need to get you up. I need you to take a shower, brush your hair, and change out of the hospital gown for me." She asked if that was something I could do, and I did it.

On the day I was discharged, I was wheeled out, and my son was still there. I just imagined him being cold and alone.

CHAPTER 2

Grieving the Loss of King

When I got home, my mom would come over to assist with cleaning and ensuring that I ate. My breasts became engorged, but I had no baby to feed. My body wasn't aware of my loss; it was ready to feed the baby that was no more. I remember having to return the breast pump that I got. The store associate said, "Is there anything wrong with it? Why are you returning it?" I burst out in tears saying, "My baby passed."

I was tormented and scared to use my own bathroom because it replayed the event of that morning in my head, so I used my boys' bathroom for a couple of weeks. I remember waking up to my husband sleeping next to me holding a picture of King that my mother-in-law Brenda had printed for us. I didn't understand it at the time, and I didn't want to see a big 8x10 photo of my deceased son, but I had to let him grieve in his own way.

As I mourned, my cousin, who worked at a mortuary, was diligently working his best so we could bury our son. My husband went and spoke with the mortuary and started the process, but they wanted me there.

King was picked up from the hospital and transported to the mortuary. My concern was that my husband Cory did not want our son "burned." However, realistically, we had no money to pay for a funeral.

I also began to get multiple doctors' bills from the hospital since I was not contracted to have our baby at West Hills Hospital. So instead of paying a co-pay, there were huge fees from everyone separately. I cried and sobbed, "I have no baby, I have all these bills, and I have no money to bury my son." So, I started thinking, and God gave me the idea to do a Go Fund Me® fundraiser.

God put our family on many people's hearts whom we had previously worked with and were currently working with at that time. My church and family assisted us with dinner, so I would not have to worry about food for my family. That was such a blessing. As a result of the 'fundraiser' and the assistance of my cousin Thomas, who worked at the mortuary, we were able to bury King. We only had to pay out of pocket for headstone at a later time.

On July 21, 2014, we buried King Josiah Sims. It took so much to just get to the mortuary. Once I arrived, my mom came and walked up to my car. She announced, "It's time to go in to the view the baby." While she held me in her arms, I said, "Mom, I can't do this." She gently replied, "Yes, you can. I am here every step of the way." The staff handed me a box of tissue and closed the door behind them so we could view our child, grandchild, King.

This was the first time I saw him since the hospital and he looked so peaceful; he looked like he was asleep. We took his picture, the same one that's on the cover of this very book, my baby.

My husband went to the baby and took a picture and kissed him. He asked me if I wanted to kiss him. I was too scared. I was afraid. I was scared to go near him. I did not want to accept the fact he was gone, but seeing him in that 20-inch casket hit home for me.

After the viewing, my mom walked me back to the couch, and I fell into her arms just weeping and holding my stomach. Instead of me purchasing a casket bouquet, I made him one with love to make it more personal, and they placed it on top of his casket. I wept and almost didn't get out of the car as the mortuary drove his body down the hill to the grave site.

When I opened the door, my youngest son Solomon came over to me and told me, "Mom, it's going to be okay. I prayed for you. It's going to be okay." I love that little boy so much as he has always had words of wisdom concerning the loss of his baby brother. We had a quick graveside ceremony, and I stayed until everyone left and said goodbye.

Now the funeral was over, what do I do? I still had the baby's diapers, clothes, and other things, and my baby was gone. I had doctors' bills and was on medical leave making less money. I was clueless and didn't know what to do with my life. My kids were being asked about the baby while I still sent them to the summer program, and it just broke my heart.

I knew of several other people who had boys or were pregnant with boys, so I gave all of King's belongings away and kept one small blanket for a keepsake.

It was time for my checkup. The medical assistant weighed me and asked for my urine sample. (Usually, you have this done every couple of weeks while you are pregnant.) I asked why she was doing this, and she said, "We have to check it for the baby." I looked at her with tears in my eyes and said, "I'm not pregnant. My baby died. Why didn't you know this?" She started to cry and said she was so sorry. She brought me into my doctor's office. My doctor came in and cried with me. She was shocked because I had a nonstress test July 3, 2014, and King did great. We talked a little more, and that was the last time I saw her.

I searched the web to see if this was common and to my surprise, this was way more common than I ever imagined. It's called *stillborn*, or medical terms *Fetal Baby Demise*. I found all kinds of group websites which led me to the Miss Foundation. I went to a couple of sessions and found it to be very therapeutic. I discovered another organization called NILMDTS (Now I Lay Me Down to Sleep) where professional photographers would donate their talents and capture the first/last moments with families who lost their children. I wish the hospital knew of this, as I would have loved to have pictures with me and my son, now that I look back.

There was a new movie released called *Return to Zero* that told a story similar to mine, but in that case, the couple didn't have any other children, and the only one they had was stillborn.

I decided that I needed to go to church and it was time. On Sunday, July 27, 2014, I asked my husband to take me, and he agreed. I secluded myself from the congregation so I would not be approached. As I was walking in the sanctuary, the greeter said, "You had the baby!" and gave me a hug. I shook my head and said he passed away.

During praise and worship a song was sung and was so relevant to my situation. "Hallelujah, you have won the victory, Hallelujah you have done it just for me, death could not hold you down, you on the risen King, seated in majesty, you are the risen King…" I stood up, still in a lot of pain from my caesarean section, and closed my eyes and started to sing and weep. I knew something had to come from this. I was too hurt;

you are not supposed to bury your kids. I actually wanted my children; why did this happen to me?

My pastor Dr. Fred L. Hodge called me and my husband up and he gave me a word, "You got a prophet in heaven and the devil was scared of him. He was horrified at what you were carrying, but you will see him. You will see him. I want you to rejoice in the fact that he's with Jesus. I want you to know you will recover all your joy. Your fulfillment will be recovered in this season, your testimony will be a word of deliverance for other women, and God will make this turn for your good. The anointing will take away all the devil structured and strategically planned. It is dissolved against you. You do have a word in your mouth and an anointing on your life. I release the anointing now - Restores, reveals, and renews, be restored in your heart, mind, spirit and soul." He embraced me, and I cried in his arms.

I made up in my mind that I desperately needed to lose my pregnancy weight so people would not ask me how far along I was or where the baby was, etc. I started taking walks at the park and sought a personal trainer's assistance to get out of the house. His name was Joseph and he did a great job in assisting me to reach my goals. I looked good on the outside, but I was hurting on the inside.

My cousin Adrianne invited my mother and me to a women's event in Victorville, California a couple of weeks before my birthday. I agreed to go. There was a woman named Jana who was the speaker, and she had painted a beautiful picture of babies with wings in the sky all with their eyes closed. I was drawn to this picture the whole time as she was speaking. After she was done speaking, I approached her and asked what the painting represented. She explained it was all the babies who have passed away while in the womb and those who were aborted by their mothers.

I explained to her what had happened to me the month before and she said, "There was a generational curse concerning my ancestors and child sacrifices." She said she was going to pray over me and that I was called to pray for babies in the womb all over the world concerning them getting here on the earth alive and well. She handed me the painting and said that it was her gift to me. I still have the picture to this day. It is a reminder that my baby is safe in my Abba Father's arms.

The day before my birthday, August 16, 2014, at about 11:00 p.m., I wasn't feeling right. I went to a local Walgreens, and my blood pressure was 180/120. I was feeling really bad and sad, and my grief was taking a toll on my health. My husband and the boys were with family. I was not ready to be out in public with anyone. I did not want to have to explain myself, what happened, or to hear some of the most insensitive comments such as, "God wanted your baby," or, "Maybe something was wrong with him." "God needed another angel in heaven." Nor did I want the looks and the stares or other pregnant people looking at me funny as if they could somehow "catch" what had happened to me.

So, at the beginning of my birthday, I was at the emergency room where tests were being conducted to see why my blood pressure was ridiculously high. I just couldn't believe all these things were happening to me. They were able to reduce my high blood pressure, and I was released that morning.

I finally started attending church after I was healed, and every first Sunday, I would sit in sorrow as my pastor did the baby dedications. I had an internal conversation with God. "Why didn't my son make it? I prayed for him while he was in my womb. I sang for him. I fasted from sweets and unhealthy foods for his health." I sought God more than ever before with this seed in my womb and was so shocked and confused and downright upset as to why God would allow me to carry this baby 36 weeks just to end up passing away only four weeks shy of his due date, literally two days after I went on maternity leave.

Back to the bills, I had multiple bills. However, God really took care of me. All the bills were waived from all the doctors. The hospital agreed to let me only pay my copay for delivery versus $1,400.00. I no longer had any medical bills from this devastation.

The holidays came up, and I was so lost. Although I tried to be strong in public, I wanted to stay at home and bury myself under my covers and just lie in bed. I had to snap out of this. I had two boys and my husband to look after. I had them as the reason to stay alive.

I began to pray. I read books of prayer and began reciting prayers when I had nothing else to say. I prayed in the Spirit, but when I sat still to hear from God, I didn't hear anything. I prayed to let me dream and to be able to see King's eyes and to see him open his eyes so I would know what he would have looked like alive, but that never happened.

I was so confused because King had words spoken over him while he was in my womb, and nothing would come to pass because he was gone. I guarded myself from people talking about my situation and had a downright pity party. I stop dressing up, stopped making an effort to do anything. I just went along with life.

It was now time to go back to work. How could I go back to a place where the last time I was there, they were wishing me well with my son and gave me a baby shower and brought me gift cards etc.? I did not want to explain what happened and be stared at. I did not want all the memories of me being pregnant there. It was not an option in my mind to stay there.

I started looking for another job and God blessed me to get an internal transfer to a closer location at a UCLA doctor's clinic in Thousand Oaks.

On a good note, God blessed Cory and I by way of Cory putting in a lot of work to enable us to have King's headstone placed right before Christmas. That was my gift, and I was forever grateful.

Mother's Day weekend was approaching. The last thing I wanted to do was hear anything about Mother's Day or celebrate it. In May, 2015, my mom requested that I join her for the Mother's Day retreat, so I obliged her and attended. I was present physically but not mentally or emotionally. I told my mom I was ready to have another baby, and she looked at me with those big almond eyes and said, "Okay, that's what I am going to pray for and be in full agreement with you," and she placed her hands on my womb and prayed over my reproductive system, my emotions, and health for the seed that I asked for.

That same day, the guest speaker prayed for me and whispered to me, "God wanted me to tell you that it wasn't your fault. The loss wasn't your fault, you didn't do anything wrong." I began to weep and sob; I fell down and just cried. It was a relief because I had it in the back of my mind that I had something to do with it. Why didn't I know something was wrong as a mother? Was I carrying him deceased in my womb all 4th of July and didn't know it?

I was just so lost, but that day I felt a heavy burden lifted. The speaker prayed for me on the last day of the retreat. She touched my stomach and told me, "You didn't even want to be here but you came anyway." She began to war over me, touched my stomach, and prayed in the Spirit. I felt the Holy Spirit over me so strongly.

On the 4th of July, 2015, my family was all calling me. They didn't want me to stay all alone. I had told my husband he could leave me at home and take the boys. I did not want them to miss the events at my expense, so I decided that I would just stay home. He went, but my mom and dad came and got me. I ended up having a good evening and was glad I did not stay home. I was feeling a little dizzy under the weather but I had a wonderful, fulfilling day. I went to bed early not looking forward to the next day, as it was the one year anniversary of King's passing.

I got up and contemplated going to church, but I just couldn't go. My mom requested that I come to her house that afternoon when she got home from church. I agreed but still didn't feel right. I had a pregnancy test in my bathroom from the previous year, so I grabbed it from underneath my bathroom counter, went into the kids' bathroom as my husband slept and my boys watched TV. I took a deep breath and took the test. My heart felt like I was having straight palpitations, tachycardia (no exaggeration). Then the test stopped blinking and said, "PREGNANT." I began to praise God right then and there. I cried, I laughed, I fell to my knees just weeping saying, "God, you are Holy, Holy, Holy!"

On the one year anniversary of King's passing, I found out that I was carrying another seed. My rainbow baby—the promise after the storm of my loss.

So many thoughts were going through my mind. I was confused and didn't know how to disclose the information to my husband and the boys. I was pondering and started asking myself several questions like, "What should I do? How would I tell my parents? Should I even let anyone know?" I sure wasn't going to display this on Facebook® since the year brought up so many memories that hurt me. I didn't know if this baby was going to make it. Would I suffer the same predicament again? I had so many questions, like a 1000 miles a minute. How will people look at me and treat me? I had to shut all those things down.

I let my friend Bathsheba know, and she gave the great idea to bake a cupcake, since that is what I do. She said to put it in a cupcake box and write a note stating, "I have a bun in my oven." So, I waited until after dinner, gave the box to Cory, and turned on my recorder. He smiled and looked and didn't get it at first with the cupcake. I told him to open the note, and he said, "WHAT!!!!!" He had the biggest smile on his face and started laughing. I then gave it to my mom and dad because they didn't know why he was acting the way he was and they both started smiling and laughing. Even and my youngest son Solomon said, "That was quick." My heart smiled.

CHAPTER 3

Pregnancy after Stillbirth

My doctors were extra careful with me. They wanted to run all the appropriate tests accurately to carry out their duties so that I did not suffer the same fate as King's stillbirth. I was scared, but I believed God wouldn't allow it to happen to me again. I was told by a couple of people, including a nurse practitioner when she saw a vague ultrasound at 12-weeks' gestation, that it was a girl. I was so relieved, because in the back of my mind, that meant it wasn't a remake of King and the baby would live and I would have a daughter.

However, when I took my mom and the entire family for a 3-D ultrasound at 16 weeks, the tech said, "It's a boy." I was shocked, my mother was shocked, my husband and boys were so excited, but they saw my face and were confused. We pulled out of the office, and my husband silently asked, "What is wrong? Our child is healthy." I began to weep. I was confused, but I talked myself into believing that I would be okay.

Cory was so excited, he posted on Facebook® and made a reference to him only making boys. I believe it was something to the effect of, "I'm like Stephen Curry. I don't miss when it comes to boys." However, the enemy tried to torment me with that knowledge as I carried the pregnancy.

Soon after that, my 20-week gestation ultrasound revealed a diagnosis of placenta previa. My placenta covered my cervix which was an alarm to the doctors. I was told I would have to deliver the baby at the 36th week. Once again, that information made me relive King's demise.

The doctors told me all the negative things that could happen, such as severe bleeding during second half of pregnancy and during delivery, premature birth, placenta separation from the uterus, which is a major problem, etc. After that moment, every time I used the bathroom I was scared and would immediately look at my tissue for blood. I would sometimes shake my belly so I could feel Anthony's movement to assure me he was alive.

On New Year's Eve, December 31, 2015, I received a call from an on-call doctor stating that something troubled her with the ultrasound of the baby's brain. I wept uncontrollably in the parking lot. I will never forget it. I couldn't go home. I went to my mom's house and my brother saw my face and said, "Who did this? I'm going to get them." I told him what the doctor said and with faith greater than mine, he told me, "He is going to be fine." I went to church later in the evening troubled and upset.

Nobody was privy to this. Nonetheless, I had to wait two more weeks before I could see her since my doctor was on vacation and was booked.

My husband and I met with the on-call doctor. She had the nerve to ask an absolutely ridiculous question, "If something was wrong with the baby would I want to continue with the pregnancy?"

I looked her straight in the eyes and said, "YES!"

I was almost 30-weeks pregnant. Did she even check my file to see I had just lost a son? She wanted to set a follow-up with me in a couple of weeks. I was furious to the point that I ignored the calls. When my doctor returned from vacation, I spoke to her and explained what happened. She had a serious talk with the on-call doctor and told her to be more empathic and read her patients' charts prior to making such ridiculous statements.

My doctor said I didn't have to worry about her comments, so I went to the follow up appointment, and nothing was wrong with my son.

I went to a service Sunday night on January 17, 2016, at my church. I was tired, nervous, and just concerned about my son in my womb. I was approaching the 36-week mark, and I was not interested in having a baby shower. I didn't want people judging and feeling sorry for me. However, I didn't have anything for my son. All of these things were on my mind.

After praise and worship, God placed me on the heart of one of the ministers, Tamara Scott, a beautiful spirit inside and out. She spoke the following prophetic word over me:

"God brought your face in front of me. Daughter, daughter, daughter. I've seen you, and yes, you have been in a valley. Even a time of valley of sorrow from the previous seed (King), many tears you have cried and turmoil you have gone through spiritually. God, how could you let such a thing happen to me, have I not been faithful? Have I not served you and yet this great thing has happened to me? Where were you God? Where were you? God said, 'Yeah, I know you have been angry with me. Yes, you have been angry with me.' And yes, you have said, 'God you've been quiet and you have not said anything that would sooth me.' But God said, 'Here you are again pregnant with a seed, but I said this is my vengeance. I couldn't talk to you about it because I didn't want you to think you could take credit for it. I couldn't tell you what I was doing. I kept you in the dark, literally in the dark, but this is my seed,' says God.

'And I trust you to raise him up. I have much work for this seed to do. I can trust you, and this is a holy and set-apart seed that would be work for the kingdom.' He said, 'Don't put him in a box. I said the kingdom not the church.' God said, 'This seed is going to transform your family and your husband. This seed is a holy set-apart seed. The tears you cried over the former seed (King) you will never cry again. Deliverance, deliverance today. No more fear, no more sorrow, no more grief. No more grief. Joy, joy, joy unspeakable full of glory!'"

My sis Bathsheba threw me a "baby get-together." She made sure there were no baby shower games. God blessed us tremendously with everything we needed for our son and so much more.

It's time! On the 17th of February, 2016, we went for the scheduled caesarean section. My mom prayed over me and the baby before they wheeled me in. After the nurses prepped me, my husband came in the room. All I wanted to hear was a cry. I needed to hear a cry.

I appreciate my doctor, Dr. Deidre Fisher. She is a true representation of not only a woman, a physician, but one who cares and treated me and my son as if it was her having the baby during the pregnancy. She made sure there were no medical resident students involved in the birth process or afterwards.

While the surgeons were performing the caesarean section, my doctor told the surgical staff and assistant to be quiet and focus on delivering the baby and not carrying on their side conversations. They honored her request, and it was silent in the room.

The baby came out, and I saw a smile on Cory's face. He went to Anthony's side, and I heard a cry. Nice strong lungs. My baby was alive! They put him on my chest, and off we went into the recovery room.

Anthony Josiah Nelson Sims arrived. He was alive. I could see his eyes. I could feel his heartbeat. He was the spitting image of his brother who passed away.

No, I am not saying that Anthony is King; he is not a replacement. He is my victory in my storm and my rainbow after the turbulence that took place two years prior. He is my happy ending, my miracle.

He is the Noah to our family who will touch our lives in many ways. God's vengeance!

Father, God, I thank you for entrusting me with this precious seed. Help me to raise him well.

CHAPTER 4

Forever King! A Strategy of Survival

"But they that wait upon the LORD shall renew their strength; they shall mount up with wings as eagles; they shall run, and not be weary; and they shall walk, and not faint." Isaiah 40:31

FOREVER KING is written to offer insight and understanding about the grieving process and perspective on how to survive the loss of unborn or stillborn children.

The information and suggestions in this book helped me heal from the loss of my unborn son, and I want to help you heal from your pain and grief. My goal is to help you heal from your grief so you can experience joy and vitality and move forward with your purpose in life.

Although the information is aimed at healing grief related to the death of loved ones, most especially unborn children, it is my hope this book will immensely benefit you and enable you to survive any difficult situation.

"Blessed be God, even the Father of our Lord Jesus Christ, the Father of mercies, and the God of all comfort; Who comforteth us in all our tribulation, that we may be able to comfort them which are in any trouble, by the comfort wherewith we ourselves are comforted of God." 2 Corinthians 1:3-4

Grief is a universal and an integral part of our life experience. It's a normal process after the death of a loved one or any type of major loss.

However, when grief is experienced, it may be overwhelming. Feelings of sadness, anger, guilt, regret, and confusion may arise. Whether we have had time to prepare for the loss or whether it is sudden, it is almost always a shock. During our grief, our world is turned upside down and we may begin to question, what is the point of it all?

Common Symptoms of Grief

- **Shock and disbelief**—Right after a loss, it can be hard to accept what has happened. You may feel numb, have trouble believing that the loss really happened, or even deny the truth. If someone you love has died, you may keep expecting them to show up, even though you know they're gone.

- **Profound Sadness**—Sadness is probably the most universally experienced symptom of grief. You may have feelings of emptiness, despair, yearning, or deep loneliness. You may also cry a lot or feel emotionally unstable.

- **Guilt**—You may regret or feel guilty about things you did or didn't say or do. You may also feel guilty about certain feelings (e.g. feeling relieved when the person died after a long, difficult illness). After a death, you may even feel guilty for not doing something to prevent the death, even if there was nothing more you could have done.

- **Anger**—Even if the loss was nobody's fault, you may feel angry and resentful. If you lost a loved one, you may be angry at yourself, God, the doctors, or even the person who died for abandoning you. You may feel the need to blame someone for the injustice that was done to you.

- **Fear**—A significant loss can trigger a host of worries and fears. You may feel anxious, helpless, or insecure. You may even have panic attacks. The death of a loved one can trigger fears about your own mortality, of facing life without that person, or the responsibilities you now face alone.

- Confusion—You may be questioning the cause of the loss. You may also wonder whether to tell others and if so, who or what. The painful grief of loss early in pregnancy is just as heartbreaking as the loss of a full-term baby. However, people often fail to reach out and give the same comfort and support or they may expect the mother to recover quickly and "try again," which could deepen your pain and confusion.

- **Jealousy**—The mere sight of a pregnant woman may cause feelings of envy. You may experience jealousy of close friends or family members who are expecting, even while simultaneously feeling genuine happiness for them.

- **Failure**—As a mother and as a woman, you may experience negative feelings about your body "failing" to carry this child to term.

- **Questioning God**—You may feel as though God is distant or doesn't care. Or you might question why He allowed such a painful experience to occur. While we don't know all the answers to these questions, we know that in the same way your heart hurts for your baby, God's heart hurts for you. He will see you through this loss and give you hope again, as He has given hope to me.

These feelings can be overwhelming when you:

- Share Your Story. Talk to your spouse, a trusted friend, a family member, or even a counselor about your loss experience in order to be encouraged and comforted. Keep a journal to record your story and feelings associated with the loss.

- Grieve Freely. Give yourself permission to do so. This may include setting up some personal boundaries with family and friends as a way of protecting yourself from people and situations that are difficult for a time (e.g., baby showers, people who tend to be insensitive, baby dedications, or christenings).

- Accept Help. While boundaries may be necessary, it is also important to let family and friends know how they can help support you. They may not take the initiative or know what would be helpful, so be sure to clearly express your needs and be open and willing to receive their support.

- Turn Toward, Not Away. Navigating a loss as a couple can be difficult as each partner tends to express their grief differently. It is important to keep the communication lines open and turn towards each other during this time. Recognizing this difference, and choosing to respond to one another with compassion and grace, will help as each of you grieve in your own unique way.

- Create Souvenirs. A part of what makes pregnant or infant loss so difficult is the absence of memories and tangible keepsakes. Create or purchase these items as a way of honoring your child who died. Some ideas include ornaments at Christmas time, a special blanket, or necklace (or other piece of jewelry) by which to remember. Create a memory box, which might include your positive pregnancy test, an ultrasound image, your personal thoughts, a poem or drawing — and designate a special place in your home for these items. Share these items with family and friends as you feel led to, which will help them to see that your child was a real baby, was valued, and is loved.

- Read Books. When I lost King, I was destabilized and was questioning God. I read so many books about stillbirths, but I was committed to a special devotional, *Jesus Calling* by Sarah Young. This devotional helped through my process of grief.

- Honor your Child. You can do so by naming your baby or doing something to honor your baby on the due date or other special days. Examples include lighting a candle, releasing a balloon, or making a donation to a related cause in your child's memory.

- Share with Your Other Children. Don't leave your other children in the dark. It is normal to struggle with the daily activities of parenting after loss. Also, don't be afraid to ask for help from grandparents, relatives, or friends. You may wonder how or what to tell your children after loss occurs. Consider their age and maturity level, then share openly and honestly what you are comfortable in a way that conveys the facts and your feelings. Sharing the story with your children will teach them about the value and preciousness of every life.

- Seek Spiritual Comfort. Approach God in prayer. Share your feelings and seek solace in Him. Read Bible verses that provide comfort and encouragement to you in times of grief.

CHAPTER 5

Suffering the Loss of an Unborn or Stillborn Child

Expecting a baby means that you're looking forward to the future. If you suffer a loss from miscarriage, stillbirth, or infant loss, your hopes and dreams are crushed, and you begin to grieve for the baby. Instead of hope, you may face uncertainty, and perhaps, a lack of support. If you lose your child early in the pregnancy or by way of miscarriage, people who were unaware you were pregnant would have no idea what you are suffering. However, friends and family members who were aware might not be comfortable discussing the loss, and/or they may not think of your loss as a death.

After suffering a loss, allow yourself time to grieve and heal. During your healing process, try not to make quick major decisions. Although you yearn for the loss of your child, another pregnancy won't replace the lost child.

Discuss getting pregnant again with your partner. Remember, the father is grieving, too. He saw you go through this and felt helpless because he could not fix your pain or the loss. Be of one accord with deciding about another pregnancy so you can walk through the next one together.

Also, please talk to your doctor. Some people decide to get pregnant right away. This is not always good for your body. Allow your body and mind to heal. Besides, if you wait the standard three months that doctors advise, you will end up being pregnant exactly when you were pregnant with your previous baby. So, take your time, and be gentle with yourself.

As believers in God, we sometimes negate storms and tragedies will come to our lives. On the contrary this will happen. The reality is, yes, we grieve, we cry, and we hurt. We are not simply dust in the wind. We are Spirit-created beings. God's very breath was breathed into man to becoming a living soul. We know our Creator, God! We are comforted by Him. As a result of His comfort, we can comfort each other.

It's important to understand that grief is a process: personal, unpredictable, and individual. The key to where it ends up is our Heavenly Father, the One whom the Bible describes as *"the man of sorrows, acquainted with grief."* When you face loss, the only answer is to seek and pursue Jesus as the chief intercessor who makes intercession for us to our Father in heaven. The Second Adam, Wonderful Counselor, the Mighty God, the Everlasting Father, the Prince of Peace.

Jesus (Yeshua) brings an ability that no theory, no description, no other person, not even a pastor can ever bring. Read this description of Him:

"Surely he hath borne our griefs, and carried our sorrows: yet we did esteem him stricken, smitten of God, and afflicted. 7 He was oppressed, and he was afflicted, yet he opened not his mouth: he is brought as a lamb to the slaughter, and as a sheep before her shearers is dumb, so he openeth not his mouth. 8 He was taken from prison

and from judgment: and who shall declare his generation? for he was cut off out of the land of the living: for the transgression of my people was he stricken. 10 Yet it pleased the LORD to bruise him; he hath put him to grief: when thou shalt make his soul an offering for sin, he shall see his seed, he shall prolong his days, and the pleasure of the LORD shall prosper in his hand. 11 He shall see of the travail of his soul, and shall be satisfied: by his knowledge shall my righteous servant justify many; for he shall bear their iniquities." Isaiah 53: 4, 7, 8, 10-11

How exactly did Jesus bear your grief and carry your sorrow? Jesus bore the cross, not only for our sins, but also for pain and grief. It describes the moment when Jesus felt the separation and feeling of isolation. Suddenly, through faith and God sending angels to minster to Him, He finished His purpose with the fulfillment of God. Take God at His word. Believe that what He says is true, even if you can't fully comprehend it. As I previously mentioned, Sarah Young's devotional, *Jesus Calling* will also help you through the process of grief.

God can turn our grief into gratitude. It may take time, but it's true. Romans 8:28 tells us that all things work for the good for those who love God. If this is your first time reading this scripture, I recommend reading, re-reading, and memorizing it.

God loves us so much that by the power of the Holy Spirit, God will heal our grief and will turn it into something that will work for the good. God can do this in many different ways. After there has been healing, we can expect the Holy Spirit will bring somebody into our lives who is also grieving. When it happens, we can be a source of hope for others because we have gone through the healing journey. *"Blessed are they that mourn: for they shall be comforted."* Matthew 5:4

Be gentle with yourself. Treat yourself like you would treat a friend; be kind to yourself. Read this daily:

"This is the day that the Lord has made! I expect to live in my purpose and receive double for my trouble! I am a precious child of the Most High God! God will deliver me and help me towards my victory! God, I trust you with my day, my life, my present, and my future! I am a survivor! I am victorious! I am a living testimony to what you have and will do through my pain! I can and will do all things through Christ, who strengthens me! The tears I've cried will be replaced with Unspeakable Joy! I will have Faith in you to expect and receive all the blessings you have in store for my life! I thank you, Father, that you hear me! That you are sending my answers to this declaration to my present! In Jesus name, Amen."

Place it on a mirror in your bathroom or bedroom. Recite it on a daily basis. This may help your healing and help you to live life again.

CHAPTER 6

The Importance of Prayer for Grieving Mothers

Prayer is important during your grief experience; it helps to build courage and fortitude.

The experience of grief may vary amongst individuals, and it is affected by many factors such as the nature of loss, past history, cultural and spiritual beliefs, and one's personality. There is no right or wrong way to experience grief. However, when we think about tragedy and loss, as much as we might want to say words of comfort, very few can actually speak to the sadness we feel on an individual level.

As Christians, however, we believe that God loves us personally and deeply. We believe that God grieves with us, mourning our loss as only He in His complete love can. We believe that God will never fail to hold us until His comfort can seep in through the darkness of our pain. The Bible declares in Matthew 2:32, *"God is not the God of the dead, but of the living."*

Although our babies are no longer with us here in their earthly bodies, they are alive, for your spirit never dies. They are happy, they are whole, they are healthy, and they are enjoying eternity with our heavenly Father! They are breathing the very breath of God. How powerful it is to know that we carried a perfect being in our vessels for the time we did. Our babies knew no pain, never knew hunger, slept well, were loved, nurtured, and carried in our innermost beings.

We know our God does not remain distant. He loves us so thoroughly that He gave us His only son. Christ took on all the weakness and pain of humanity. He also wept at the loss of His friend Lazarus. He gave Himself on the cross that we might rejoice with our loved ones at the heavenly banquet, where every tear will be wiped away.

The love of Christ has triumphed over every evil, even the evil of death. Even as we can perhaps see that hope for the future, we also know that Christ does not stop there. While we have to wait here in our sorrow, Christ accompanies us, holds us in His loving arms, and brings us strength and consolation. We shouldn't forget that we are the Body of Christ, and as a community, we can use our members to wipe away tears and embrace one another. There is nothing more endearing than human connection and interaction when embodied with the Holy Spirit.

Talk to Him about the loss of your child. Ask questions. Cry before Him. Become intimate and consecrate yourself. Pray, and praise His name, because He is our forever love, and He will definitely wipe our tears.

When there are problems and challenges in your life, do not be overwhelmed with anxiety. Scripture encourages us to *"pray ceaselessly"* in times like these and ensure that your "petitions be made known unto God" 1 Thessalonians 5:17; Philippians 4:6. The Bible assures us that if we pray to the Almighty God, even in times of grief, *"And the peace of God, which passeth all understanding, shall keep your hearts and minds through Christ Jesus"* Philippians 4:7. We can gain a measure of tranquillity by pouring out our concerns to God. In fact, He encourages us to do so.

"Therefore take no thought, saying, What shall we eat? or, What shall we drink? or, Wherewithal shall we be clothed? 32 (For after all these things do the Gentiles seek:) for your heavenly Father knoweth that ye have need of all these things" Matthew 6:31-32.

I faced a lot of challenges since my experience of King's stillbirth. I was really scared during my subsequent pregnancy, but God saw me through. I was relieved of the burden, and by God's grace, I have the power to endure. By virtue of prayer, I am able to go through my daily life with fewer worries and with a conviction that God will take care of me. *"Cast thy burden upon the LORD, and he shall sustain thee: he shall never suffer the righteous to be moved."* Psalms 55:22

Are you facing extreme grief, perhaps even life-threatening or tragic circumstances? Praying to the God of all comfort can bring immense relief. The Bible says that He comforts us in all our trials.

"Fear thou not; for I am with thee: be not dismayed; for I am thy God: I will strengthen thee; yea, I will help thee; yea, I will uphold thee with the right hand of my righteousness." Isaiah 41:10

For instance, on one occasion, when Jesus was greatly distressed, "He bent His knees and began to pray." The result? *"And he was withdrawn from them about a stone's cast, and kneeled down, and prayed, And there appeared an angel unto him from heaven, strengthening him"* Luke 22:41, 43

Another faithful man, Nehemiah, suffered threats from evil people who tried to stop him from doing God's work. He prayed, "Now, I pray, strengthen my hands." The subsequent events show that God really did help him to rise above his fears and to succeed in his work.

My experience with prayer (Placing Request Accessed by Yahovah Expecting Results) has been that when I pray, especially in times of trouble and overwhelming difficulties, I get a firm conviction that I have told someone who has the means to help me and who assures me that there is no cause for alarm. Yes, God can grant us everlasting comfort when we pray to Him.

CHAPTER 7

Studying the Word of God

How can you find comfort when you have experienced the loss of a child? This is a very practical question that deserves an answer. I am one of four women who has experienced stillbirth which prompts the inspiration behind this book. Scripture does not specifically address the subject of how to cope when you experience the loss of a child. However, this does not imply that God is silent. Scripture has much to say regarding how to think about, cope with, and respond to all the different trials and pain in life during your time of grieving.

I am not saying that it will be easy. It will be tough. You will have to strengthen your will to praise, to pray, to travail through this storm in your life. This is so true because the flesh would like to dictate your life. You cannot live solely on feelings and emotions as they do not know your future, your purpose, your destiny, or your end! Do not let the enemy dictate your praise! God is working in your life so powerfully that you will be able to do far more than simply cope with your pain.

The first question a grieving mother may ask is, "What is the eternal destination of my baby?" My son is in heaven awaiting our reunion. He is very much alive, and I will see him again. I will see his eyes! Don't allow the enemy to make you think God took your baby or that He wanted an angel in heaven. God's will is not for children to die. However, there is a time and season for all things to come to an end. Unfortunately, death comes sooner for some than others.

There is no passage or verse that is clear on the subject. Scripture does say that God is absolutely sovereign and absolutely good. It is clear in every page of God's word that He is perfectly holy and just. The Bible also says that God is full of mercy and kindness. Seek the comfort of God through the Scriptures.

When you lose a child, the pain is nearly unbearable. This pain transcends physical pain. The very essence of this pain comes with lost opportunities, such as birthdays, time, hugs, kisses, laughs, and lives shared. It is isolating darkness where there was once warm light. Losing a child leaves a vacancy in your heart and makes you think you simply cannot go on. After a loss of such magnitude, how can anything ever be the same? This vacancy in your heart is so large that no one and nothing can fill it except God.

There is an emotional pain in your life that only the Father of all comfort and compassion can mend and start to heal. *"Call unto me, and I will answer thee, and show thee great and mighty things, which thou knowest not. Behold, I will bring it health and cure, and I will cure them, and will reveal unto them the abundance of peace and truth."* Jeremiah 33:3, 6

"Have not I commanded thee? Be strong and of a good courage; be not afraid, neither be thou dismayed: for the Lord thy God is with thee whithersoever thou goest." Joshua 1:9

"And God shall wipe away all tears from their eyes; and there shall be no more death, neither sorrow, nor crying, neither shall there be any more pain: for the former things are passed away." Revelation 21:4

"I waited patiently for the Lord; and he inclined unto me, and heard my cry.

He brought me up also out of an horrible pit, out of the miry clay, and set my feet upon a rock, and established my goings. And he hath put a new song in my mouth, even praise unto our God: many shall see it, and fear, and shall trust in the Lord." Psalms 40:1-3

CHAPTER 8

God's Sovereignty in Times of Grief

The question, "Why did this happen?" leads the Christian to consider what is the nature of God's relationship to the death of His son (Jesus Christ).

God gave His son for us, knowing He would live again, and we can have that same assurance and peace. We will also be raised by the Holy Spirit on that great day. We can rest in His peace.

"And the peace of God, which passeth all understanding, shall keep your hearts and minds through Christ Jesus. Finally, brethren, whatsoever things are true, whatsoever things are honest, whatsoever things are just, whatsoever things are pure, whatsoever things are lovely, whatsoever things are of good report; if there be any virtue, and if there be any praise, think on these things." Philippians 4:7-8

When you experience something as devastating as the loss of a child, you will inevitably want to blame someone: yourself, the doctors, or God. I need you to hear me when I speak this over your life, when you read this statement and get it deep down in your spirit, in your soul, and in your mind. As previously stated, know that it is not your fault.

The selfless act of choosing life for your seed, carrying your child in your womb for the short period of time that you did is such a beautiful thing. You held your seed their entire life. Your baby wanted for nothing and only felt the love and compassion you were able to experience with the child. God knows your end from the beginning and everything in between. He has made sure that absolutely everything that has happened, including the great loss you have suffered, has not happened in vain. Be encouraged!

Let's look at the wonderfully tailored historic events of Joseph. God clearly orchestrated all the events so that Joseph would be separated from his Father. He was sold into slavery by his envious brothers who lied and said he was killed by a wild beast. He was falsely accused of attempting to rape his master's wife, and he was thrown in prison. Finally, after many years, he was given a position of power in Egypt under Pharaoh. Imagine the years of suffering that Joseph experienced—the pain and loss that his father had to endure.

The reason why all these events transpired was clearly beyond their grasp for many years. Yet, when Joseph was finally able to confront his brothers who had caused so much pain, he had an understanding of God's intentions in all the pain and suffering experienced: *"But as for you, ye thought evil against me; but God meant it unto good, to bring to pass, as it is this day, to save much people alive."* Genesis 50:20

God's plan was to make Joseph a vessel that would help through the period of famine by storing grain for survival. For many years, neither Jacob nor Joseph himself could have possibly made heads or tails of why a good God could have brought so much pain and suffering into their lives, but God had an amazing and good purpose from the beginning.

Remember, He is aware of the end from the beginning! Consider the greatest evil ever committed—the crucifixion of Jesus Christ. This was the cold-blooded murder of the only innocent person in the history of the world. It is recorded in the pages of Scripture as an evil act that men are blamed for and an act that God himself willed to happen. *"For of a truth against thy holy child Jesus, whom thou hast anointed, both Herod, and Pontius Pilate, with the Gentiles, and the people of Israel, were gathered together, 28 For to do whatsoever thy hand and thy counsel determined before to be done."* Acts 4:27-28

Simultaneously, it was a crime committed by sinful men who conspired to do evil. It was an event that was decided beforehand by God and caused by His power. Consider the amazing fact that the greatest evil ever to occur is also the greatest good! As we work through difficult issues and situations in life, we must remember to trust God and have faith (Fearlessly Alleviating Ignorance Trusting Him).

"And we know that all things work together for good to them that love God, to them who are the called according to his purpose." Romans 8:28

God will do a new thing in your life concerning the recovery of grief to live and continue to live for not only yourself but those who are still living that need you! *"19Behold, I will do a new thing; now it shall spring forth; shall ye not know it? I will even make a way in the wilderness, and rivers in the desert."* Isaiah 43:19

When you don't know what to say or can't speak, God will receive your tears as prayers. Imagine as you cry, the angel assigned to you bottling up those tears and ascending into heaven and pouring them on your book of life. As they are poured, see the words being formed from your mind, heart, and soul onto those pages. Revelation! *"Thou tellest my wanderings: put thou my tears into thy bottle: are they not in thy book?"* Psalms 56:8

God will give you double for your loss. *"I will go before thee, and make the crooked places straight: I will break in pieces the gates of brass, and cut in sunder the bars of iron: And I will give thee the treasures of darkness, and hidden riches of secret places, that thou mayest know that I, the LORD, which call thee by thy name, am the God of Israel."* Isaiah 45:2-3

Wait on the Lord, listen for his still voice. He has your future ready for you. *"14Wait on the LORD: be of good courage, and he shall strengthen thine heart: wait, I say, on the LORD."* Psalms 27:14

In the midst of your pain, praise Him! God will come for your praise. He will receive it. *"And one cried unto another, and said, Holy, holy, holy, is the LORD of hosts: the whole earth is full of his glory."* Isaiah 6:3

Decree and declare positive affirmations and other scriptures into your future concerning all areas of your life. I am at peace. I am healed from grief. My heart is no longer heavy. I hear the chains, falling! *"28 Thou shalt also decree a thing, and it shall be established unto thee: and the light shall shine upon thy ways."* Job 22:28

CHAPTER 9

The Experience of Joy as Commanded by God

Joy Experienced after Grief

The second step in gaining comfort is to recognize that joy is a command by God. He commands every believer to always stay joyful. *"Thou wilt shew me the path of life: in thy presence is fullness of joy; at thy right hand there are pleasures for evermore."* Psalms 16:11 This is very different from a command to always be happy. When I refer to joy, this is neither a superficial smile nor a carefree attitude. Christian joy can be accompanied by tears of sorrow. Christian joy is a satisfying mood or feeling, which motivates one to live for Christ.

The source of joy is hope and trust in the goodness of God, in what He has done, is doing, and will do. If you have lost a child, there will be days when your sense of loss will be almost intolerable. But it will be accompanied with an abiding trust in the goodness of God and what is to come after your loss—a perfect, satisfying, and comfortable ending.

How do you Derive Joy from Despair?

The third step in gaining comfort from God is to begin working hard at transforming your mind. We have just learned some truths about the life of a Christian, who God is, how He works, and the way to respond to your suffering.

Now, I want to show you in practical terms how to get from despair to joy. If you have lost a child or suffered pregnancy loss, you are most likely in a sea of despair. You may wake up each morning trapped in memories of what was or dreams of what could have been. Begin to renew your mind with the truth in Scripture:

"And be not conformed to this world: but be ye transformed by the renewing of your mind, that ye may prove what is that good, and acceptable, and perfect, will of God." Romans 12:2

Actively work at replacing thoughts about the unfairness of your situation with thoughts about God's perfect and good purpose being worked out in your life. Fight the good fight of faith.

Replay in your mind and constantly recite 1 Corinthians 10:13: *"There hath no temptation taken you but such as is common to man: but God is faithful, who will not suffer you to be tempted above that ye are able; but will with the temptation also make a way to escape, that ye may be able to bear it."* Concentrate on how you might love other people to the glory of God.

When others ask you about your loss or show concern for you, thank them and tell them what you are learning about God. Be honest about your struggles. Consider how Christ has shown you tremendous love by laying down His life for you, and then you begin to lay down your life, your preferences, and your comfort for the sake of others. You will see that once you begin to pour yourself into other people, your life will begin to inch towards perfection. You will find your way from despair to joy in Christ; hence, it can be achieved through constant study of the Word of God.

CHAPTER 10

The Intervention of a Support Group

As a mother experiences grief, it takes divine intervention to have peace of mind and travel the path to healing.

However, one of the steps I took during the loss of my unborn child was to visit support groups. The symptoms experienced from grief were overwhelming, but the support and encouragement offered were extremely comforting. When you've realized the symptoms of grief that threaten your health, decisive actions should be taken to mitigate such effects.

- The most important factor in healing from loss is having the support of other people. Even if you aren't comfortable talking about your feelings under normal circumstances, it's important to express them when you're grieving. Sharing your loss makes the burden of grief easier to carry. Wherever the support comes from, accept it and do not grieve alone. Connecting to others will help you heal.
- **Turn to friends and family members** – This is the time to lean on the people who care about you, even if you take pride in being strong and self-sufficient. Draw loved ones close rather than avoiding them, and accept the assistance that's offered.

Oftentimes, people want to help but don't know how, so tell them what you need – whether it's a shoulder to cry on or help with funeral arrangements as I did for King.

- **Draw comfort from your faith** – Have faith in God that everything works together for good. Do not subject your faith to doubts because doing that will never let you find comfort in the sight of God. Spiritual activities that are meaningful to you, such as praying, meditating, or going to church, can offer solace. If you're questioning your faith in the wake of a loss, talk to a pastor, intercessor, or others in your religious community.

- **Join a support group** – Grief can feel very lonely, even when you have loved ones around. Find a support group you can join, get books to read, and pray ceaselessly as Scripture instructs. It is important to understand that sharing your sorrow with others who have experienced similar losses can help.

- **Talk to a therapist or grief counselor** – If your grief seems too much to bear, call a professional with experience in grief counseling. An experienced therapist can help you work through intense emotions and overcome obstacles to your grieving.

Ask for help when you need it. There are trained professionals who can help you with the healing process. Asking for help is a good thing, and God desires to bring healing into your life.

Surround yourself with those who will support you. Remember that you do not have to do this alone; God did not intend for anyone to be alone. You will smile again. There is a happy ending to your current storm. Pay it forward, and bless others going through your same situation, showing them that you can live. Life will and must go on. God knows the thoughts and the plans he has for you.

Here are some thoughts to help you prosper and bring you to your expected wonderful end.

You are fearfully and wonderfully made. You are the apple of His eye, your very existence was already written and designed before you were born. There is a plan for your life. Expect the best! Be blessed!

Forever King

I wonder who called an angel, why you chose to volunteer;
Your short life given in sacrifice, a King's move
For one of our members you hold dear.

I'll never figure why you've left us,
Will never ask the question for whom
I'll just say if it be me you chose to protect,
We've got problems, 'cause I'd have simply traded me for you.

I didn't catch your name, but a stranger, no not to me,
Pure in heart and in spirit you chose to go
So, I'll call you, forever, King
Were all in a bit of pain right now, knowing not the job you
Chose to do, knowing not weight of our decision, or
The very essence of your suffering, our time being due.

Please know even we feel, there's no blame,
Even in sorrow Mommy and Daddy think so, too.

I didn't catch your name, but a stranger, no not to me,
Your life you gave and through death you live,
So, I'll call you… Forever King - *Uncle Robert*.

Acknowledgements

To Danielle, my prayer partner, I appreciate your obedience and heeding the Holy Spirit's unction to give me a word to pursue this book and share this story. Keep those prayers coming!

Bathsheba, you are my sister. You were there for me at the lowest point of my life. Thank you for your presence during this storm. I am so grateful that after my loss; you made a selfless decision to choose Cory and me to be the Godparents of your baby girl! I love you to life!

Shanea, My long distance Sister! We met one month after I lost King. We connected instantly and stayed in contact through my grieving process. You sent me beautiful scriptures, text messages and the very book "Jesus Calling" that kept me sane and not giving up on life. You are a beautiful centerpiece to a tarnished world. Let your light continue to shine bright like "Platinum Diamonds! My dear friend tragedy brought us together and God has and will get us to His Perfect Peace!

Erica, My Birthday Sister! One of the most real women I know, I thank God for you! You have greatness overflowing in you. Use your mouthpiece and charismatic influence that God gave you to impact the world! I thank you for being here for me, hugging me, feeding me, laughing with me. The best is yet to come.

Roxy, My Latina Sister! Always smiling. You are truly an overcomer of major adversity! I prayed for you and your handsome babies and you in turn remembered me. You made sure I received a text from you every day for months to make sure I was okay, to make sure I know you were there for me. I will never forget you.

To all who were there for me and my family, thank you!

About the Author

Diana Sims is a Survivor. Her passion is helping other women continue to live while grieving the loss of their children by early loss in pregnancy, miscarriage, stillbirth, or infant loss. Diana's transparency will inspire and help you see the light at the end of the tunnel or a new beginning from the previous end.

Diana's convinced that the pain she experienced with her loss positioned her to reach the masses and show that things can get better, marriages can survive, and families can, as well, grow and heal.

Diana is committed to humanitarian services, whether in her field or her personal life. She worked for many years helping customers keep their homes from foreclosure during the economic fall in 2008. Currently, she is assisting physicians and patients as a Patient Liaison. Diana is a California native and resides in Southern California with her loving husband Cory Sims and her three handsome Kings in training: Isaiah, Solomon, and Anthony Sims.

Stillbirth Statistics and Causes:

Stillbirth is classified into early, late, or term.

An early stillbirth is a fetal death occurring between 20 and 27 completed weeks of pregnancy.

A late stillbirth occurs between 28 and 36 completed pregnancy weeks.

A term stillbirth occurs between 37 or more completed pregnancy weeks. (2)

Stillbirth affects about 1% of all pregnant women, and each year about 24,000 babies are stillborn in the United States. That is about the same number of babies that die during the first year of life, and it is more than 10 times as many deaths as the number that occur from Sudden Infant Death Syndrome (SIDS). Most causes of stillbirth remain unknown. Many times, doctors would perform autopsies on the baby and still no cause would be discovered. Cacciatore and Collins came up with a term in 2000 called "sudden antenatal death syndrome." this term is rarely used, but it exists. In other cases, however, the cause of death of the baby is known, and these are some of the causes:

Bacterial infection

Birth defects

Chromosomal aberrations

Growth retardation

Intrahepatic cholestasis of pregnancy

Maternal diabetes

High blood pressure

Drug use during pregnancy (nicotine and alcohol)

Postdate pregnancy

Placental abruptions

Physical trauma

Radiation poisoning

Rh disease

Female genital mutilation

Prolapsed umbilical cord

Monoamniotic twins

Umbilical cord length - A short umbilical cord (<30 cm) can affect the fetus in that fetal movements can cause cord compression, constriction, and ruptures. A long umbilical cord (>72 cm) can affect the fetus depending on the way the fetus interacts with the cord. (4)

Cord entanglement—This refers to when the body or neck of the baby is wrapped in the cord causing restriction in the flow of oxygen and blood. These situations can be detected with ultrasound.

Torsion—This refers to an umbilical cord that is twisted up. The average cord twist is about three twists.

Source: Journal of Investigative Medicine

http://jim.bmj.com/content/55/1/S129.3

Bibiliography

1. "Miss Foundation" "https://http://la.missfoundation.org/common-questions". Retrieved 01/17/2017

2. "Facts about Stillbirth" "https://www.cdc.gov/ncbddd/stillbirth/facts.html" https://www.cdc.gov/ncbddd/stillbirth/facts.html. Retrieved 01/17/2017

3. "Fetal and Perinatal Mortality: United States, 2013", Marian F. MacDorman, Ph.D., and Elizabeth C.W. Gregory, M.P.H., Division of Vital Statistics

4. "Stillbirth"

    "https://en.wikipedia.org/wiki/Stillbirth" https://en.wikipedia.org/wiki/Stillbirth. Retrieved 01/17/2017

5. Journal of Investigational Medicine: 324 "Demograpics and obstetric correlates of stillbirth in a large urban population."

    S. Rad, D. Ogunyemi. "http://jim.bmj.com/content/55/1/S129.3"

www.ingramcontent.com/pod-product-compliance
Lightning Source LLC
Chambersburg PA
CBHW071743040426
42446CB00012B/2461